THE LOST PROV

Poetry by Thomas McCarthy

THE FIRST CONVENTION
THE SORROW GARDEN
THE NON-ALIGNED STORYTELLER
SEVEN WINTERS IN PARIS

Thomas McCarthy

THE LOST PROVINCE

ANVIL PRESS POETRY

Published in 1996
by Anvil Press Poetry Ltd
69 King George Street London SE10 8PX

This book is published with financial assistance
from The Arts Council of England

Set in Bembo by Anvil Press Poetry
Printed and bound in England
by Morganprint (Blackheath) Ltd
Distributed by Password, Manchester

ISBN 0 85646 276 4

A catalogue record for this book
is available from the British Library

TO
KITTY COAKLEY

ACKNOWLEDGEMENTS

To the following magazines, where poems have previously been published: *Force 10*, *Iowa Review*, *Irish Times*, *Krino*, *North Stone Review*, *Poetry Ireland Review*, *Rhinoceros* (Belfast), *Southern Review*; and the anthologies *Jumping off Shadows* (Cork University Press) and *The New Younger Irish Poets* (Blackstaff). 'The Garden of Sempervirens' was originally published in *Poetry* (Chicago).

The author gratefully acknowledges the assistance of the American Irish Cultural Institute and the Arts Council, Dublin.

CONTENTS

PART THREE: *Why the Earth is Calm*

PART FOUR: *Declan, Scientist*

PART ONE
Love Medicine

THE GARDEN OF SEMPERVIRENS

We've been in this small room since daybreak.
I look out on America, sunlight on the great plain
of a neighbour's roof, an Ojibwa spirit
racing by. We lie at ease for our own sake.
The frenzy of late March or a nineties puritan
need for work can't move us from our perch.
You do move your arm, grown a little numb
from the weight of me. We both talk of home

and how we must go back. But for now
we are as numb as a young prisoner in Portlaoise
who hears these words for the first time, *amnesty*, *ceasefire*.
At five thousand miles we manage somehow
to find a new vocabulary for peace.
Peace, like light, is almost too much to bear.
After so many years, how to come into the sun,
pull the harrow from the brambles, set to garden.

From this bed where we made love I can see
more than a few winter creatures basking in light.
A College mower goes by, but squirrels hang on.
Late March America is theirs completely;
all ten thousand lakes and a thousand islands.
Our own life has the sandalwood vapour of night
marked with the fresh touch of your mouth,
love and story, the accent of the South.

Yet what I might have written was suspended
the way yard-work is in a Minnesota winter.
We held our breath. Now, see the winter heads of Clematis
the winter colour of Bergenia, or Skimmia,
with its white panicles of fragrance, up-ended.
We see again the private lust of poems and paralysis
of poetry in a time of war; and how, undeterred,
Buxus keeps its shape, year after year, *in memoriam*.

PRISONS

for Catherine

You walk across the compound on a clear day,
the morning damp with dew –
dawn like a squad-car carrying you
away from me. I watch the way
you walk, elegant as usual,
into the new prison school.

Out of one prison into another.
Last night the determined prison officer, our son,
poked at you with the warm baton
of his bottle, his eight-ounce *Pur.*
There's no escape from the love
he has cast about us, and no reprieve.

You were so free when I first saw you
ten years ago. When you walked
(no woman ever had a walk as bold as yours)
out into sunlight from the pub door,
I hand-cuffed you into talk,
I was your holiday inquisitor.

Embarrassed eyes gave you away.
While others pleaded I held you on remand,
my fingers touching your hand.
You withheld your address. But today,
today, you walk through the new prison gate,
your scarf beside me like a half-sheet.

PICNIC

The afternoon glows with self-conscious beauty.
A layer of rowan-berries falls across the sunlight,
rows of orange montbretia, fuchsias becoming trees.
Heather and fields arc out of sight

when we park the car in a rutted drive.
We picnic in your mother's abandoned yard,
a cottage at the end of unbearable decades.
A decorative place. How easily we discard

the personal life of a whole generation.
This was the essential home of a big family,
a priest in Martinique, and, at Cappoquin Station,
an uncle bound for the fire-service in LA

– saver of money, cashier of Atlantic passages.
It is no myth, but sociology!
The poor here suffered an awful tetanus.
Today you offer me profiteroles with salmon pâté.

The world suddenly is a more descriptive place,
not just the place itself. Each wine-glass
has a watermark, its crystal light on your face
is money refracted. The farmyard wears a designer

blouse of whitewash. An old bucket blushes
to find us more articulate and over-fed.
The earth has moved. Without us paying heed,
the sun got through to cobblestones and bushes.

DAMAGE

A ferry-boat returns with damaged trucks.
The ocean is indifferent. Recriminations come ashore
like small damaged cars.
The car park sees a homecoming of wrecks.

The ships owners called it an act of God:
a freak wave caught the ship unawares.
But the irate passengers, the drivers,
scream about unsecured loads,

irresponsible sailing, grim weather forecasts.
Four couples were on their honeymoon, outward
bound for France. They had barely turned
to each other when the freak wave crashed,

a wall of sea against their frail arms.
Two couples weep now as they listen
to the loss-adjuster. He says there are worse
fates in marriage than small damaged cars.

TRADE LIKE LOVE

A Cuban ship is turned in the harbour.
Its great bulk moves tentatively like marriage.
Two infant tug-boats pull against its weight,
their motors dig into the churning water;

the hawsers sing. The ship ends its passage
in a cacophony of rubber and steel plate.
Buffers squelch. Containers catch the sun;
they advertise their exotic origins –

it is trade like love that begins in promise.
Great shipping lines keep trading to avoid ruin.
The Lloyds bell tolls for voyagers gone down.
Receivers gauge their catastrophic losses

as we measure the balances of love and pain.
Beloved, the emptied ship rises in the sunlight.
You cross the room to look. The plimsoll line
made by your pantihose is level with my eyes

when you stand beside the chair. My lips
touch your skin. Your indelible fingers
stroke my hair. Love registers the Cuban ships.
It makes a chandlery of tide-charts and cigars.

A NAVY SKIRT

A wet and house-bound day at the end of July:
we meet briefly and kiss
among the coral islands of old clothes.
You are clearing the wardrobe. Life's come to this,

this vital reassessment in the encrusted ocean
of our bedroom. A navy skirt lies on the floor
as it lay years ago near a glass of wine.
A purple tie-dyed blouse is torn

from your life. The scattered black and green kelp
of tops and trousers, frayed sweaters, that were
part of my love for you are helped
into the oblivion of black bags. The shore

is littered with your former selves. Lovers
I touched have been consigned to dust, to sand
and water. I knew your moods by their textures.
Your changing patterns I watched, to understand

which good moment to ask a favour. So much
was granted in the licence of clothes: sex,
a soul to speak with, anecdotes against loneliness.
Now the ocean takes all your polo-necks

and lace collars. The ground is littered
with the left-overs. You've fulfilled the chore
of coming into focus. You offer, again, a brief kiss.
Whole futures surge in to your tidied space.

HERE YOU ARE

Stranded for hours at Belfast Central
I have time to look again and again
at three photographs in my breast pocket.

How fragmentary life is! How powerful
images are that cut into us like shrapnel.
Images push forward against loneliness.

Here is Pasternak, a photograph
brought home from Russia by poet friends:
here – after the riots – is the poet,

all birch trees, cornflowers and carnations.
And here are my two brothers, a small
black and white photograph I took in 1968

or '69. They are playing with a terrier
in the Cistercian field. Kevin is laughing –
the baby, we are proud of his intelligence.

And here you are, lost in contemplation
on a Kerry beach. The sea is behind you,
breaking gently at the centre of my heart.

Your check skirt billows in the wind,
a squall catches your hennaed curls.
This love we carry is a telephoto lens.

HONEYMOON PORTRAIT

What survives is an image of you
as youth on the brink of some new distress.
Neither the raw carnivals of Paris
or *fin de siècle* ironworks break through

to allow for celebration. Your distant
look, your eyes that went dark with boredom,
constantly escape from the cheap bedroom
of tourist art. Your anecdotes rinse

the romantic hogwash out of moonlight.
Wait, who mentioned the moon?
Give the moon a break. The highly strung
Vietnamese exile has a perfect right

to paint the moon or dissolve the moon
to suit the purpose of her loaded brush.
What murderous B-26 crushed
her native studio and made her a Western

portrait painter? She chokes now in the lacquer
factory of Paris. She is one more displaced
woman, bombed out with her mother
from the Asian delta. The chalk she placed

to her lips was sulphurous with napalm.
Between you two there was a resonant mantra:
a prayer excluding men. You shared tourism
of the globe and the female body. I saw

the look of exile in her trapped eyes.
She caught the look of a honeymoon in you:
how no intelligent woman could subdue
the loss of territory that a marriage means.

NOVEMBER

The sun has burned the toast of the morning
yet again. Outside our window, late mist
is blown upriver. A thrush begins to sing;
it spits through the flaky Saturday haze.

In the yard there isn't much left of autumn.
Frayed Virginia leaves in the corner
are the summer's disquieting shrapnel –
one year on, an Arts Council grant winds down.

Life that is fragmentary and difficult
has had space to run with outstretched arms;
the blame and lack of love you might have felt
is deeper now. Our child bawls like an alarm

as he has done every night for two years.
Has he found me wanting? I would not wish him
the father I had; hopeless father
who couldn't shield us from the bitching parish

of his own misery. The house was claustrophobic
but only with his own troubles.
It takes so long for a father to learn love,
to ditch the hero for the outstretched hand.

We survive self-knowledge like the memory
of war or a car crash. Not only ourselves
are victims but those who teach us to love.
Each year vanities fall away like leaves

to expose more of our basic structure,
all lopped branches and cankered scars.
Here is memory, here is the recent humus
of trouble. The new gutter sheds tears.

Each gust of wind traps more retreating leaves,
keeps them cornered, makes a damp imprint
of whatever wound. The full year grieves
like a bomb-victim in a basement

and poems come like ballads of the IRA,
under pressure but not admitting love;
primed to defend the hot selected areas.
There, time stands still, more naked and unkind

as years pass overhead. In the shopping mall
of parenthood we are lost. There are fractious walks
in the park, tired shoulders in a wood
or seaside strolls where once was horny talk

before love-making. These, the recurring images
of you, seashells, stones on a sunlit beach,
dolphins, these come to me at the edge
of autumn. They are out of reach

too often now. Pressure of the domestic,
ritual duties of the house. We yearn for more:
domesticity is only interim music.
Love feeds at the edge beyond the seashore

from where it springs. Leaves brush against
the breakfast window. You are asleep once more
after a night of lustful happiness
stolen from the kids. Let's get a divorce

from them and hide in the foliage. Toast
is burning for you through the breakfast news.
The purple dregs of wine in a glass –
Californian, and ripe as figs

against a November wall – have not lost
their sexual taste. The night was seed-filled
and hot as any night in adolescence.
The deep tannin of love still holds.

Only poetry itself is ever autumnal,
wanting to drag in and to store too much.
Better to lose as much again, overturn creels
of possible images. One cannot store touch

or the sensuous moment. The year hangs
now from the cliff of autumn. Winter fills
us already with its compositions, its strange
cleansing light. Rain has washed window-sills

and left them gasping. The haze has lifted.
I breakfast on the good words between
us now. Winter arrives with its gifted
techniques. Leaf fragments adhere to glass, seem

like marmalade pieces left on a plate
or sweet-papers blown across a beach.
I move to the grill to turn up the heat
for more toast. Sunlight is within reach

if only I could touch the lintel of November.
Familiar smells, the grill-pan warms.
November, your birthday. Love breathes upon fear
the way a kiss moistens an exposed arm.

LOVE MEDICINE

Sunlight falls on the April drinking vessel,
evening sunlight like an Australian pearl-shell.
A bumble-bee flops from its winter dream-time.
Persistent birdsong animates the fetus.
I watch the children at their ancient rites,
the ritual avoidance of brother and sister –
Kate determined to avoid the levirate;
Neil, with his kangaroo-skin headdress,
negotiates the tribal ochre of azaleas.

Old prams, tyres, shreds of earthenware
are residue of the owners who once lived here,
dreaming their unfinished lease, their firesticks.
Remnants accumulate when I sink the spade
while our own children go walkabout,
bound for the interior, full of love-magic.
We watch their heads disappear in the fresh earth
while the sun flings deadly stones of heat;
light drunk with fragrance from their birth.

SNOW

Cold palette of winter on the narrow lane.
I park the fat beige tube of car and walk.
Kate's hair, like a wayward streak of Titian,
cuts through the pure viridian of air.
We jump to avoid the soluble blue
of an Opel, a strong Prussian intruder.
Our hand link across the bismuth white
of packed snow. Without speech,
warm in the encrusted seal of her lips,
we catch the blue of a child hurrying indoors.
A nod of acknowledgement, a thumb raised,
delicate as camel-hair, she disappears.
Suddenly, the brilliant tincture of a child's laugh
from the euchrome of the cloakroom.

Daughter, your lips are too sore to kiss now;
your cool face, titanium white of inert snow.

AN EXCHANGE OF GIFTS

for Denis

We are here at the edge of the known world,
arriving at Easter to exchange gifts of chocolate.
You have been walking among the medieval laurels
with my wife. The children play on a black gate,

chasing the new watch-dog, inventing names
for things they haven't even touched. Red
of frosted camellia and flowering crab
catch the light. Evening is a watery Pieris.

You talk together as if talking to some part
of me; which is what love is, how it should be.
During these terrible weeks she has been my heart.
A Geraldine officer, you know about anxiety;

territory lost, foreign wars, brothers in trouble.
It is wrong to gain too much at once –
you look back and see things diminish, castle by castle;
just our organic life is left, then nothingness.

We step indoors to exchange small gifts.
Eggs in silver wrapping accumulate.
Still, they are more than good manners. Votive,
they are candles of one kind of faith.

Your mother's carriage-clock chimes. I listen
to its prudent reminders. Wars and fathers
break through the silver-wrap. The children scream
with delight. They gambol across the hours.

Timeless barbarians, they won't behave.
Egg-shaped, noble, life is at the table's edge
while a child goes by. What we are sure of
is memory, with its blue and gold Fabergé.

THE LEINSTER FITZGERALDS

for D.H.F. on his 80th birthday

I know you hate the cult of birthdays –
for yours came at the wrong time of year,
three weeks into a new term,
and all the loneliness of a boarding school.

The trees you've planted have kept your secret:
Amalancier leaf-spears, overflowing Bourbon roses,
colour the page of days into a greeting.
The equinox blows its eighty candles,

quickly the smoke is claimed by the bonfire.
Years open like courtyards at Carton –
your ancestors come onto the terrace to cheer.
There's Emily, the Duchess, and betrothed

in early youth. There's the whipper-snapper
young Jacobite and his Pamela de Genlis;
there, behind her, walking from the farrier's yard,
is the Great Earl himself, and Garret Óg.

What a party! No expense is spared.
The trees have put out their best spoons,
the lawn is a broad heraldic carpet.
Birds run through the usual brass tunes.

– And still your day is a secret.
Except in the encumbered estate of the mind:
there, long wax candles burn for you. Your name
is spoken. There's a Humphrey Lyttleton band.

AUSTRALIA

for Martina and Brendan

Wool falls like a tumbling kitten.
You finish the last row, frantic with exile,
and tack the sides of a child's blue jumper.
Sheets are folded. A king-size tablecloth

of stiff damask is wrapped in tissue.
You fold the clothes of your unborn children
without sentiment, but fiercely private.
The pride in your fingers is detailed.

Australia has caught in your throat like fever,
love-fever, something from adolescence.
The removal men have compressed your adult life
into cubic yards. If Australia could

only see you now, getting out of Ireland,
it would raise its reefs with welcome.
Oz is the Camelot you've been waiting for
– *Qantas* the wild lover and groom.

A TEACHER HAS DIED

in memory of Rita Hogan

'Say *wagness, wagness* for the Irish word.'
The word for loneliness was often on your lips,
and the pallor of O'Riordaín, his white face,
our greatest dying poet. In the absurd
moments of a school syllabus you wept
with the poets. Classroom mystic. 'It is no disgrace
for people to weep in their poetry.
Tears on the page can help us to see

our own unhappiness more clearly.' Our childhood
was already beginning to fall apart
when you arrived, nervous as a seabird,
out of a Gaeltacht we little understood.
You were always giving assignments, paragraphs
that piled up uncorrected. You needed to hoard
our second-rate ideas. When you died
they died with you, ungraded at your side.

CUMANN NA MBAN

You were sixteen. Your desk at lunchtime
was an impromptu Irish army dressing-station.
Your satchel hanging from the radiator
was a blue UN flag. You were assigned
to heal your men, and they moved closer
and closer. That classroom was full of pain.

Lipstick and *Spotlight* magazine. A jar of lies.
Your long sallow hands on the trestle-table –
healer with big eyes, sad as Jack Lynch,
though your stunning looks never stood idly by –
you fed the wounded while you were able.
Boy-soldiers were given a tablet of talk each

and ordered back to the front-line. They left
without protest. You were their Jubilee nurse
as well as the officer in charge of lust.
It was your hazel eyes and various besotted males
that locked in combat. Heroes, in happy disgrace,
had you picking shrapnel from their chests.

BEGINNING WITH A LINE BY DON DELILLO

A series of frightened children appeared at our door
for their Hallowe'en treats. Autumn again,
scavenger of expired grasses and scarlet.
October blows its saline vapours.
Maple leaves twist and scar in suburban rain.
The year swallows daylight hours. Interiors create
domestic or literary happiness; time is vying
with the centre of our lives. Used books
pile up against the squirrelled staircase,
collect at the half-door of the heart.
Each competes for attention like a tired child.
The lair of the house is leaf-lined and half-lit.

Wind blows like a shut-out child on the street.

TRISKEL ODEON

Another film-club Saturday. Lights down.
The screen lights up to show its fabric art.
We sit quietly in the Triskel Odeon,
watch a director bare his serious heart

with the heating up too high. There is sweat
already on my buttoned-up shirt.
The projector fulfils its whispered threat
and breaks down. Suddenly dreams fall apart

as quickly as they're projected. I wait,
with one hundred other adults, for noise
and light to begin again. At this rate
we'll never have our weekend blast, our money's

worth of foreign films and sin.
We shift uneasily in our directors' chairs;
wisecracks, as diffuse as light through muslin,
fill the air. It's back again! There's

a rush of sunlight, the healing Mediterranean.
If only our small towns could have been like that;
if we could rearrange and splice the frames
to make a new milieu, begin with something white

instead of sleet on St Patrick's Day, or Fianna Fail.
Someone blew the projector bulb of our childhood,
leaving a wet, grey street. No *Amarcord*
to talk about, no olive trees; no cinematic light.

THE CLASSIC CINEMA

The yellow JCB, a roaring Schwarzenegger,
thumps and buckles a ton or so of brick façade.
What was once a cinema is now lunchtime traffic
through a hole in Washington Street. Walls fade

through a grey filter. The Classic becomes vapour
in the time it takes to fill a belly with soup.
Bricks are dismissed like so much popcorn;
liquids spill from the straws of old pipe.

The crane-driver, like an impatient usherette,
hurries two purple radiators along.
Stubborn in their seats, they screech and fret,
then exit finally in a heated exchange.

Remember when we sheltered behind the glass doors?
And the musty dampness of November Sundays;
bone-bare toilets, a porter's housecoat
rotting in the corner like an abandoned corpse.

Each exposed frame gives way completely.
The projection-room fireplace gapes at the sky,
watches openly the last blue movie –
the producer's lover gets ready to die:

a demolition ball and chain arcs above me.
Awkward memory leaps from the torn balcony seat;
it lashes out like a B-movie pirate
but falls among accountants, box-office receipts.

DESMOND CINEMA, CAPPOQUIN

I sit with John Crowley in the projection room
of McCarthy's ambitious Desmond Cinema.
There is the flapping sound of a reel's end
that John has been rewinding for return.

It may be a film from Paramount
like *We're No Angels* or *To Catch a Thief*
(I think it was Cary Grant's face
that passed us by on a damaged frame).

John has been here since before I came
into the undirected world of waste and death.
Cappoquin, 1960. He's projected light
over the heads of those left in town –

their bodies writhing under the higher etiquette
of Hollywood as well as Church and State.
I wish I could unreel the many sounds
that lulled our backwater of happiness:

the silver tones of Nelson Eddy's throat,
the weak-kneed mush of *GI Blues*,
the alarming hooter in *How Green Was My Valley*,
and music from *The Song of Bernadette*

that haunted mothers who couldn't emigrate.
John, spools click in the empty auditorium.
You strap tightly the aluminium film box,
send dreams like emigrants on the 4 o'clock train.

THE PORTUGUESE VOYAGES

Another perfect luncheon at Casa de Mateus.
The afternoon is held steady on brass gimbals
of vines; the frantic swell of autumn.
A bumble-bee, adventurous Vasco da Gama,
strikes southward from the Cape Verde
of a pear tree. The air is heavy with cloves
and cinnamon. This garden is indomitable enterprise.

The sun extends its empire westwards –
Malacca of shadows, Goa of heat, Angola of tears.
The sun drops its logline over the fretwork pergola.
Still the most important voyage in history,
daylight searches for life in the globe of leaves.
Pears swell like the industry of love;
eastward a tractor sails, an ancient caravel,
its rigging disappears into the horizon.

Portugal engulfs me with its soft brown eyes.
Water is its element. Look, these Portuguese voyagers!
They break from the treaty of a late luncheon,
bearing cross-staff and astrolabe of words,
their vivid vellum portolani.
They voyage beyond the comfort of house linen,
while I, transfixed, bond with the nearest sod,
touching earth and its immutable hour-glass.

PART TWO

The Lost Province of Alsace

THE NEW EURO-ROAD

Election posters in the winter rain. The car
like a magic carriage brings me back –
attendant mice, rodent footmen –
roads tending clockwise in the winter clock,

time won't run out until we get back.
Rain falls in the principality of brown cows.
Rain cascades from the luggage rack.
Water has primed the November hedgerows.

We can never get back to the first surface of home.
From the new EC road – raised above flood-level
with German money – I can see the river-side street
where I was born. I can hear the church bells.

The town cowers like an exhausted father.
Everything has changed. We were never closer to Bonn,
or Milan or Cologne. We were never closer
to a fairy tale. Heartbroken afternoons at home

now seem like details from another biography.
My past has the texture of an Italian film:
to be seen fully certain blinds must be drawn down
against the light, and talk kept to a minimum.

Misfortune flooded my childhood so many times.
It's good to see it now from a raised Euro-road.
Would I go back? Would a donkey go back to the mines?
Would a salmon return to a lake without food?

POLLING DAY, 1989

Another hot day at the end of the campaign;
not a crowd to fill my punishment-cell library
or the distant tennis-club polling station.
I lunch in the shade of an ugly sycamore tree

and watch the drying straws of a late June.
A Green Party van chugs by, emphysemic,
rattling in the potholes of our Republic.
A Fine Gael woman walks from her blue BMW

to show clothes any mortal would vote for.
She is tanned with the confidence of her class,
gifted, walking with purpose. A red Labour poster
vies with the black-rimmed borders

of Sinn Fein. A government car
speeds by, raising dust in the blistered street;
its tinted occupant is blissfully unaware
of sycamore, dying library or summer heat.

I finish my sandwich and fold the cellophane
of my lunch-hour into a tight ball. The hard
mahogany of the bookshelves beckons. No rain;
sycamores drop their unwanted polling-cards.

THE COUNT CENTRE

Once again, the aleatory ballot-box.
Franchise clerks tumble dice across the table.
Power has broken its seal.

Trestle-tables are loaded with wads of votes;
candidates chew their Cuban pencils.
There's a call for order.

This is the tense time of dealing out –
a tallyman grumbles quietly, a clerk
moves away to make room for lamplight.

The tables are littered with wild returns,
a shift of emphasis, a weird transfer.
Eyes strain to see what an opponent has.

Hard necks are stretched.
This day is beyond us, beyond words.
All, at once, are triumphant, wretched.

THE WAITING DEPUTIES

Tonight I drive through my native county.
Ten o'clock, all the canvassing over,
the lights go out in the last polling booth.
Incumbents await their final transfer.
What is it that my childhood meant to say,
I wonder? Just one version of the truth

will out tomorrow when seals are broken.
I drive through the latest interregnum
as November rain drove through here for weeks.
Posters lie torn in the exhausted towns
of Dungarvan and Lismore. The rain-storm
of polling day has abated. The night speaks

to me like an old detective –
it protects the boxes and seals power.
Who will be responsible for my childhood
when the votes are counted? Where
will the blame fall? The way I live
now prevents any party from looking good:

what I write, remember and feel,
excludes me from their well-connected world.
When I was poor these men did business
as if nothing happened. I was told
they had power to attend to: they used to sail
in and out of our demented terrace.

The unopened boxes will see me right.
My parish sleeps on its pillow of votes.
Cappoquin, between river and the trees,
ignores its grumbling questioner, its poet.
It sleeps upon favours. In the calm of night
they wait with me, the would-be Deputies.

SNAP ELECTION

The Party men have failed you in three colours.
A councillor tells stories. You sit beside him
in desolation. It is the spring of 1973.
You bend your head like a jilted lover.
Television light flickers across the room;
a neon hunchback with a threatening broom
that spits upon you and empties ash-trays.
It repeats figures and mentions the weather.

You move your legs reluctantly and brood.
Never blame a higher power, never.
It's the local district that brings failure.
You moved in the small arena, three townlands
at most, and no more expected help from Dublin
than from Christ. There are Party men you loathe
who failed to deliver the budding votes.
You bind the voters' lists in an elastic band

and raise your whiskey to a term without power.
A more hostile Dáil will eat your liver.
Death will catch you in its snap election
before the decade ends. Provoked by television
you walk away into the post-election rain,
avoiding candidates – the four failed names
as if they had committed some crime against
a bleak betrayal of family, a desecration.

POLLING DISTRICTS

Midsummer thunder has made the sky clear –
lounging clouds have been for a long walk.
The skylight picks out abandoned registers,
shredded by the teeth of years. Pencil-marks
of young personation officers start
to burn off in the light. A Tupperware
jar of indelible pens is canvassed
by a party of spiders, a microphone of chalk
breaks through to dominate the plastic soapbox.

Sunlight gnaws the floorboards where they lie,
dusty now and naked, and dog-eared.
So much power has gone quiet; its weird
and remarkable loss is a mystery.
I can almost hear the pages cry
although the attic-boards creak and resist
any perfect silence. Crouched low, I try
to arrange old polling districts in a neat
pile. Pages are smudged with my father's sweat.
I think of his red hand on those voters' lists,

a hand that was absent so often from our house.
He had to canvass too many other places,
neighbourhood terraces, walls for notices,
not to mention drunken election crowds.
But these abandoned registers, the lost quires
in our attic, are my keepsakes for 1977.
Nothing less than his indices of heaven,
they decay more quickly every passing year.

SHROUD

The Taoiseach's face comes into grey focus
like the lately usurped Turin Shroud.
His speech is barely audible. The distress
of failure cannot be hidden from the crowd.

Crumbs are thrown at the gasping press corps;
images to fill up the emptiness of days,
gossip to feed that hunger. Running scared
at the nothing in our lives, we praise

a photographer's tit-bit. Flashbulbs tell us
what we already know. It's been a tough
campaign; power has suffered a hair-loss,
the Taoiseach is ill, tired, becoming rough

with those who question or disagree.
The helicopter gunships of the canvass
have left unbearable ringing in his ears;
a cynical decompression has taken place.

A bulb flashes like a fresh blood-stain.
What is it that keeps him going?
Is it power only? The sacred? The Shroud of Turin
that fills our man with the Jesus thing?

Is it that some Deputy might touch the hem
of his Government and become important,
or some dark Magdalene
wipe perspiration from his face. Can years

of anxiety fall away? Photographers hint
at nothing more than mortal grace, his tiredness.
Television, our daily linen, leaves a quick imprint.
Elected Christs disappear without trace.

THEM HISTORIANS

for Donncha O Corráin

There is a lot of pride in the words 'mere
historian'. So don't give me that crap.
It's a tactic to shoot down the high-flyer
young poets, so see them end up with egg
on their texts. Each of them devours the sap
of the past. You hold the keys of the keg-
room, though. You store the meat and mead.
Poets only travel where the archives lead.

MICK HANNIGAN'S BERLIN WALL

Your wall, Mick, fragmentary and dry
like a crust of burned soda bread,
has travelled across the snowy American
country. Your wall has become my daily bread:
more real and sacred
than a piece of the True Cross could be,

and more transcendental than poetry.
Daily I go to the Communion of plaster
and feel its stinging flakes.
I wonder how many demolished homes
went into its making; the holy sepulchre
of Berlin torn apart and emptied

to be reconstructed as a mere wall,
a miserable, miserable wall. One people
were divided and terrified. It was, someone said,
their just punishment –
as our divided island is a just thing:
perfect image of the spirit unwilling.

Mick, I divided your wall in Syracuse.
No, not Syracuse. It was Burlington, Vermont.
I gave it to a poet during a snowstorm.
A divided Sacred Host. I thought guilt
and history are divisible like Grace.
He thanked me as one thanks a priest.

THE LOST PROVINCE OF ALSACE

I SPEECH

That June afternoon, drinking near Grafton Street
after your father's speech in the Dáil,
we fell into conversation
with two Catholic girls from Tyrone.
Their fingernails were still lightly chipped
from hanging off the ledge of the North.
They were full of emigré hope and gratitude.
They had both landed jobs in the capital.
Dublin had opened. They had season tickets.

I mentioned the Beef Tribunal, the 'golden circle',
the ten-year betrayal of the unemployed.
They would have none of it.
Dublin had opened and they had season tickets.
It was you who mentioned the old Senator
in the Dreyfus affair, Scheurer-Kestner –
after 1871 he chose to live in France
but kept his eyes open, read all the documents:
in this way never lost the province of Alsace.

II NATIONAL TREACHERY

Our neighbour's son, a teacher's oldest child,
lay down beside me in Deputy Glenville's field.
We spent whole days looking at the sky,
wondering what held it up, wondering why

it was always blue. He became so concerned
about the sky that he fell seriously ill.
Professionals counselled him through the term.
He avoided me when he came out of hospital.

The big questions never troubled me as a child.
Questions dissolved inside me like vitamins.
I fed upon them. I was solitary and spoilt.
Yet there was one recurring question: it burned

a hole in my heart. Afraid to ask friends,
it went unanswered. I'm alone with it still.
Why was my father powerless, and all my cousins?
What treachery did we commit against the Dáil?

III CITY OF ROSES

The people who were happy with Stormont
loved roses, or so you insisted.
You travelled north in late '64
to sell steel gates to men who wore
metal Union Jacks in their lapels.
Lemass's voice was ringing in your ears:
'If thine eye offend thee, do business.'
There were McGredy roses everywhere you went.
It was a city of roses, it was.
You bought two H.T.s for your married lover,
hid them like contraceptive devices.
Long after, their grit stuck to your clothes;
and bits of a wet *Newsletter* that covered
their thorns, their hybrid Talmudic pages.

IV AT PORTLAOISE PRISON, 1993

It is time for the lighting of lamps,
sancte venite, the coming of night.
Portlaoise prison, custodial hands
are placed upon ceramic light.

Republicans retire into their cells,
certain I have left unfinished
the long ambiguity of poems.
I leave the scriptorium, a list

of scholars and heroes in my notes.
Gracious, the monks have given me a gift
of tooled leatherwork.
Generous they are, even as they resist

the flux of liberal ideas:
they give what it is their minds make.
The monastic code is precious.
Their view of history is what takes

some time to understand. It lacks
a medieval world. For poets may come,
luminous with ambiguity,
gifted as *filí,* welcoming Englishmen.

V TALKING TO GERRY ADAMS, 1994

We are three floors above your foot-soldiers,
which is the right of those who exchange ideas.
We know nothing about fuses:
we detonate opinions and views.
Your handsome face (the face of Sean Moylan
in Keating's *Men of the South*), has no pain
visible to me. It has absorbed politics,
and flying columns of documents.

Today it's the 'productive atmosphere of peace'
after war. I find myself switching sides
already. Maybe this is what poets are for
in a destitute time. To stay apart
from the Dáil. Thinking finds a Protestant in me;
and Ulster, an autonomous region of the heart.

PART THREE

Why the Earth is Calm

If it was a train only, it wasn't at this small station

It was one of those five afternoons
in Paradise. A bone-dry day,
nettles and parsley on the embankment.
A train pulled out of Cappoquin Station.

The earth moved, and the train
like an elephant spitting through the trees
beat me from the ticket office. Was it
Jackie Greene, the phlegmatic clerk,

who flagged it back again?
I can't remember. But I recall my foot
on the grey, moulded pedal-step
and the feel of a master's hand at my back

pushing me on. The August afternoon
carried me drunk to Dungarvan.
Even then I knew I'd used one day
out of the four or five in childhood.

It is risky and primitive, it is an unhappy childhood

Images of grief take time to be formed.
Only now I've learned to handle our father,
his meticulous, minutely organised idleness.
He stood in our childhood corridor,
a depressed face-painter, painting stress-
lines. Our mother, busy and inarticulate,
looked on as we queued to be crayoned.

Yet he had such sweetness of character –
how many times did our mother fall asleep
in his arms? He held up the tent of the night
with his stories. He triggered our mother's laugh.
Sometimes her laugh was heard on the street.
Their love was clairvoyant and deep:
nothing that happened could touch it,

not even us. A day went by in their life,
it was only one day, it was risky and primitive
as love is a chance and a bond
that gives the weak courage. One day a wife
walks indoors with her strange new husband:
who knows what ghost will touch their lives?
Fate will hold them in the palm of its hand;

it will blow upon them, cold air
from the letter-box, furnace of the bedroom.
Still, their crises primed us with feverish hands;
them licking crayons for our hearts' thin paper.
Depression was an art-supplier.
Their memory is a tear-based pigment. Words form,
again and again, to speed its aphaeresis.

A photograph of the Ranga*, it is curled at the edges like memory*

I've pinned a picture of the *Ranga*
to my office door. Six thousand miles
from home tall young Seniors
stare at the frightening wreck:
it is their *Pequod*, their *Patna*.
The black incisors of Coominole snarl
back, the Atlantic foams at the mouth.
Water pours from the oceanic spigot.

This week we dedicated to images
(third week of the fall semester),
images both abstract and concrete.
I think of the work to come, Emotions, Memory,
and present this wreck, hope they feel it –
deep enough for an attitude to form.
The sea has burned the *Ranga* with oxides,
no dry parts where paint might hide.

But hold it a minute, wait your turn!
It's not a wreck, a rusted bridge, I see
but the day when the photo was taken.
The *Ranga* is biography washed by the sea,
our love life. It is a photograph
of the finger that pressed the button:
the clever wreck that captured us
all summer: the *Café Liteartha*, coffee.

It is easier to deal with Yeats,
it is easier without thunder

This desolate and hopeless thunder.
Each of us earns our living
hardly looking up to see the lightning
arc between chapel and national flag.

The classroom is stifled with promise.
Against the weather, our Yeatsian arguments.
September flings a continent against us.
Twelve tired imaginations stir.

So where were the Leninists when I needed friends, when I needed summer?

August has stretched its toes into September;
hot-blooded August staying alert with bees –
a late flourish of roses on its toenails.
Butterflies inoculate the pink buddleias.

September can't catch them in its brown net,
nor can water from the lawn hose catch them.
They barrel across the garden yet
like so many disentangled yellow roses.

1991 turns like an old wooden globe,
or something more animate, not made of wood;
a huge creature pinned down by strings of hope,
casting fortuitous shadows, crying for food.

The children play in its outstretched petals.
My wife sleeps in its tanned breast.
September gives her the novel of revolution:
mystical reading is the aria and chorus.

It is poems I bring to assuage his melancholy,
anecdotes from the bourgeois life

Your father gazes steadily through the window.
The world looks in at him and guesses.
Melancholy has given him a peculiar foothold:
books wash quietly from the bourgeois world.

They settle at his feet. Ah, he has just missed the boat,
just by half a government. If he'd been in the Party then,
if his intelligence had learned to negotiate,
he might have come home to a political welcome.

Instead, he is powerless in his working-class island.
Reading has set him apart. He doesn't understand
that books are like dead voters, an embarrassment.
Melancholy has gripped his beautiful, trapped heart.

Believe me, it's worse to witness anger
than to meet it head on. It's more like fiction

The sun on impulse lifts above Cappoquin, throws
light upon your father's endogenous depression.
It is middle age in the adult world.
Sunlight falls upon the libido of trees

and sets the world chattering, chattering.
Birds, like so much grain, lift from the weighty earth,
become a shower skywards. The kettle is singing
in the mother-lit fireplace. Your mother

has risen at dawn to be before you.
Her steady gaze now is what holds us together.
Gone the happy politics, the health of friendship.
He is no more a man, but the absence of one.

Your eyes are on the light from the window,
the morning paper-round, obligations made clear.
You leave the house, but your mother has still to listen.
She grumbles quietly in the district of fear.

I think of the fathers I've invented,
and marvel that the earth is calm

I watch from my father's meadow
the outgathering of swallows.
They mince the light afternoon –
a ratatouille of shadows
oiled by the falling sun.
Autumn flings them across trees and wires,
specks of life go lighter and higher
until snuffed by the peregrine

of distance. The earth is more calm.
It's immovable, even warm
compared to cold ideas in the sky.
A rock-rose comes to little harm
down here, a scandent jasmine, white-eyed,
feeds off the last humus of summer.
Petals heave at the least murmur.
August settles old scores at my side.

Here things are different and the same:
different since our children came
and moved us back a generation.
Being in the world is less pain
since they waved their mystical arms.
Ideas are no longer migrant
only, but rooted to the land
that constitutes their names.

It's love that marched them through the trees
to check engines that might have ceased –
too many ideas, cloudbursts, rains,
rusted life, left us diminished.
Sunnier now the wear and tear
that calms my dread, implosive anger.
Their fragrance falls across our knees.

I watch more swallows bank southward.
Early evening still, the air is cold
already. Michaelmas stretch their green fists
from the Senecio carpet. Untold
stories lodge in the pampas grass.
From here I can hear their gossip;
watch politicians take malicious shape,
each pulled by the tropism of disgrace.

I think of the terrible mistake poets made
who attached themselves
to Marx instead of their fathers.
Laws of light and leaves
cannot be altered. Green corridors
of natural law never submit.
Philosophy bends to sunlight
and seasons. Earth is umbilical of power;

and nothing so puritan, so man-made,
as dialectical secateurs
can sever the bond with the dead.
And this belongs to all. Others,
behind whichever Balkan wall,
often luxuriate in loss.
I recall Bloody Sunday. You recall
Enniskillen. Corpses lie on our flowers

while we think and talk and watch.
We marvel at the conference of swallows.
I gather a few myrtle logs
from your winter pile of lime and larch.
Their bark is the colour of blood
myrtle cut from its natural home
and left to die. Through it, be understood
the ironic warmth of the war poem.

It is Stormont, it is the Dáil
that makes an awkward, distant Hell-
place where swallows go to browse.
Truth is only a kind of petal
blown against the wall of each house.
It is power, it is powerful men
I've interiorised. They leave me troubled
and uprooted in my father's garden.

PART FOUR

Declan, Scientist

DECLAN, SCIENTIST

Super aegros imponent manus et bene habebunt

I BBC GAUL

The sea lives in constant amazement
with itself. Our grey promontory,
our business park that natives call
the monastery, or monastic settlement,

can never outshine the sea.
Its harvest is welcome but tragic.
Even I myself have felt
(like followers of the Patrick cult)

the sea's desperate loneliness.
Were it not for the radio at night –
BBC Gaul, Fluctus-Brevis News, Radio Lux –
I might become a wind-torn anchorite.

II THE HEATHEN GODS

Today we learned about the heathen Gods,
gods of water and earth. But especially Brigid,
a kind of foundress Mary Baker Eddy,
whose cloak of prayer covered acreage

bigger than our business enclosure.
God showed displeasure through her
with boils and sores. The land reveals itself
thus, layer by infected layer.

III FALL

Leaves scatter in our healing park.
Wind blows the untreated parchment
of summer. The stripped bark
from our charcoal fires
flutters in the west wind.

Another summer as Christ's instrument.
Time flies. Twenty little gurriers
are rescued from the Patrick cult.
Clear signals on the 30m band
and these, psalms on all four winds,
Fall's blessed diatesseron.

IV FEATHERS

The teeming bird-life of the Patrick cult:
all these blackbirds of the enclosure
like the tears of octopus on parchment,
loathsome Celtic ousel and robin.
The elder Julius has been up since dawn
laying down poison:

such a cloudburst of the feathered dead!

V GALILEE

Not for us the bleak last supper
of the suffering Patrick cult,
rather the joyous morning picnic
with the risen Christ as exemplar.

We are flattered by Princes of the Deisi
bearing gifts; filigree gold
for melting down to micro-chips,
complicated Pictish MSS

and a white-haired Princess.
We gaze upon this beautiful daughter
of an unsaved Celtic chieftain –
gold nor God-health will move her.

VI MOCHUDA

I pray for Brother Mochuda's wound.
It festers and grieves in him.
Pain is more than a memory with him
since he fell from the short-wave aerial.

God be good to Mochuda
who tried his best to receive news from Gaul
on the thirty-metre band.
Mochuda, native Gael, you broke your back

while searching for God. The elders
love you. All the elders from Cappoquin
have prayed over you. Even the wind howls;
your radio mast takes the strain.

VII AD 435, AUGUST

Another day of aching heat –
grass high and stiff as a donkey's rod,
the sea a looking-glass.
Brother Mochuda's been sharing God
with Patrick's victims.
Alas, there's hardly grain or meat
enough for a healing colony.

'Brother,' I said, 'I know it's August
and the first roots will soon be lifted,
but there are too many mouths to feed.
Why don't you return to the broadcast Christ.
Radio has such influence . . . Just for a month.
DXers have less physical needs.'

VIII LOVE

More dynastic quarrels in the North.
A pall of smoke is visible on Sliabh Gua.
How unlike happiness smoke is,
how it contains a false warmth of fire.

Mochuda has been pining for the fair-haired
Princess. He suffers. He has fallen
into that malicious animal magnetism.
We have been praying against his grief,

this woman who has ensnared him.
But he seems not to want relief.
All day he looks north to the *Rian Bó Phadráig* –
erotic ambush on his damaged brain.

IX BOSTONIUM

Come in! Come in!

It's the Mother Church, Bostonium.
Brother Mochuda is frantic for news.
The waveband, narrow as gallium arsenide,
is difficult to hold. 'Don't lose
us!' he yells from the scriptorium.

Poor Mochuda. He fades. Last night
he saw a young woman bathed in light.

X ST DECLAN'S STONE

A minor prince refuses to see the light.
'You!' he screams at me 'are people of no background!'

Their genealogies are full of horse-shit –
as if a man were no better than his birth:

M. Rosa,
M. Nair,
M. Fiachair,
M. Conaill,
M. Mecar,
M. Oengusa.

When I came over the sea from Gaul
on a boulder of coarse gritstone
I came with one father only, Christ.
The well-begot comforter.

New and Recent Poetry from Anvil

12